READ ABOUT

THE HAND

written and illustrated by
KATHLEEN ELGIN

FRANKLIN WATTS, INC.
575 Lexington Avenue
New York, N.Y. 10022

For Joady

Library of Congress Catalog Card Number: 68-11205
Copyright © 1968 by Franklin Watts, Inc.
Printed in the United States of America
by The Moffa Press, Inc.

1   2   3   4   5

READ ABOUT
THE HAND

Your hands are remarkable tools; tools which
do many hundreds of important things for
you . . . things you don't even have to
think about.
They can pick up a puppy.
They can grip the handlebars of your bicycle.
They can stroke a kitten's fur.
They can make a snowball.

Your hands are your workers.

They can open a book or an envelope.

They can make a dollhouse or throw a ball.

They can close a door and then turn the key.

The touch of your fingers can tell you the
difference between the smoothness of an
eggshell and the fuzziness of a peach skin.

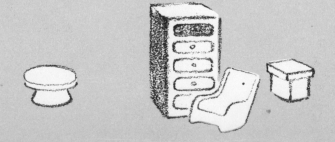

Your hands can hold a violin and its bow.
They can touch the 88 black and white keys
of a piano to make music.
They can take lumps of clay and mold them
into a bowl or a little pot.
They can take a brush and a palette of colors
and paint a picture of something you like.

Many parts of your hands work together to accomplish these little miracles — bones, muscles, nerves, and blood vessels.

There are 27 bones in the wrist and hand.
The 8 small bones in the wrist form the joint
   between the arm and the hand.
They fit into the 19 hand bones.

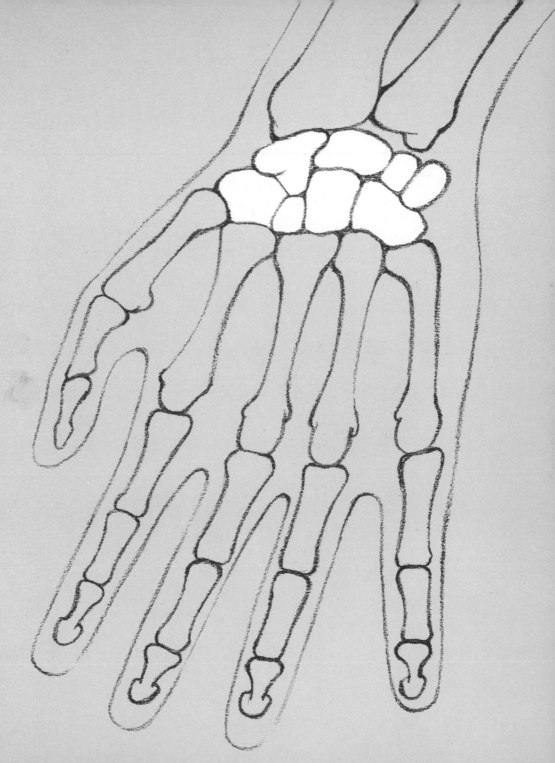

There are 5 bones in the palm of your hand.
These hand bones connect with the thumb
and finger bones.
One hand bone connects with the thumb
bones.
The other four connect with the finger
bones.

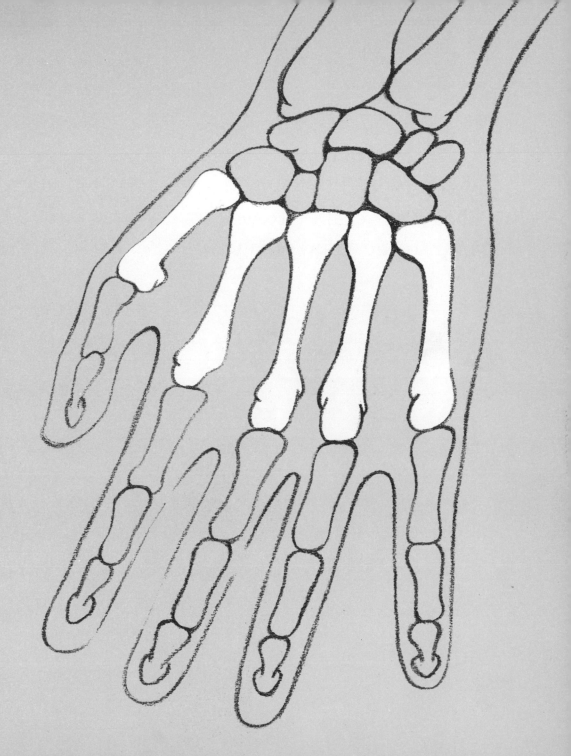

Your thumb has two bones and each finger
  has three bones.
All bones of the fingers are constructed alike.
The longest and strongest hand bone leads
  up to the middle finger.

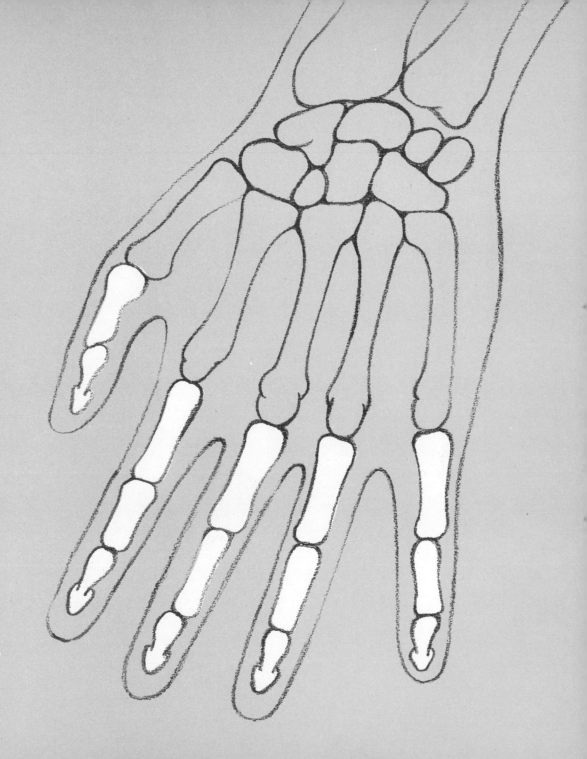

21

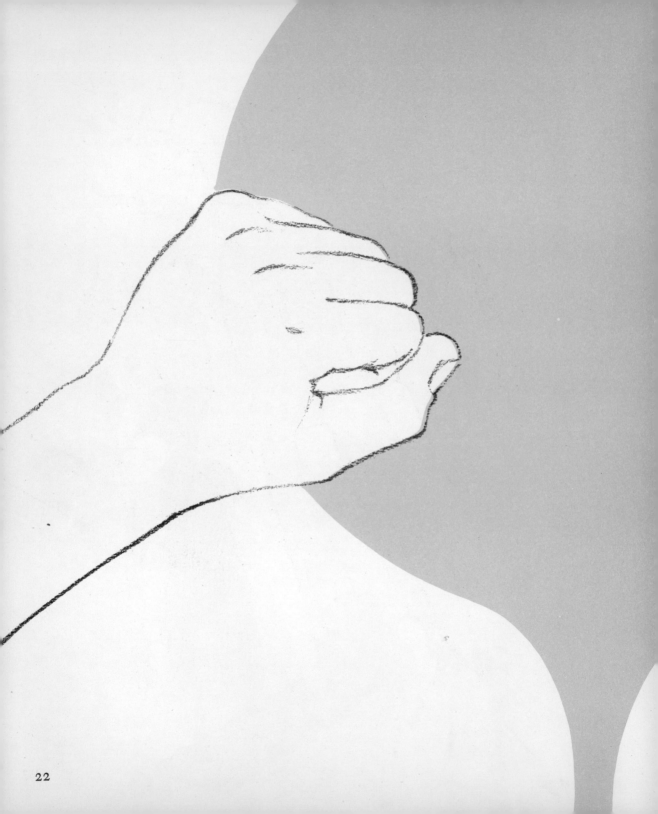

The ends of the bones fit together solidly,
   like parts of a puzzle.
Your knuckles are formed by the joints of
   the finger bones.
You can see your knuckles quite plainly
   when you make a fist.

Your hand can become a delicate instrument
   too.
The tips of your fingers can pick up a thin
   thread, and then put that thread through
   the tiny eye of a needle.

Man's ability to use his hand in a hundred different ways makes him superior to the lower animals.

In addition to the other abilities that set him apart, man is the only one to have this great advantage.

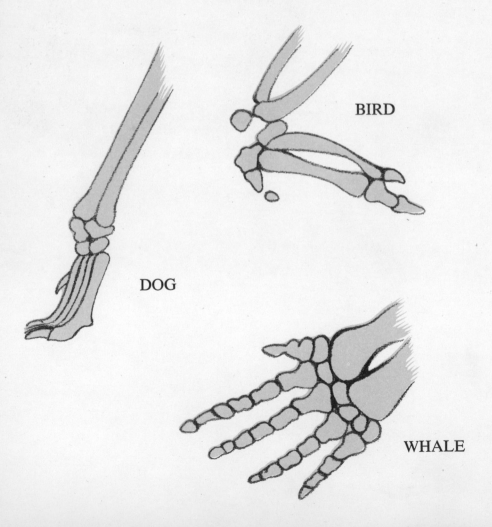

BIRD

DOG

WHALE

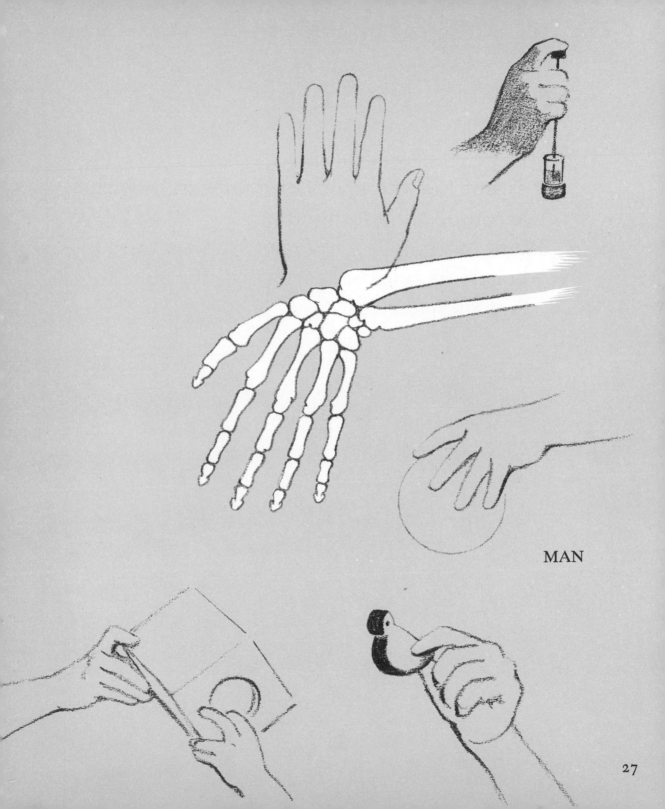

MAN

It is not just the bones of your hand which
accomplish these things.
There are muscles, too, which move the
bones; muscles of the fingers, the thumb,
and the palm.

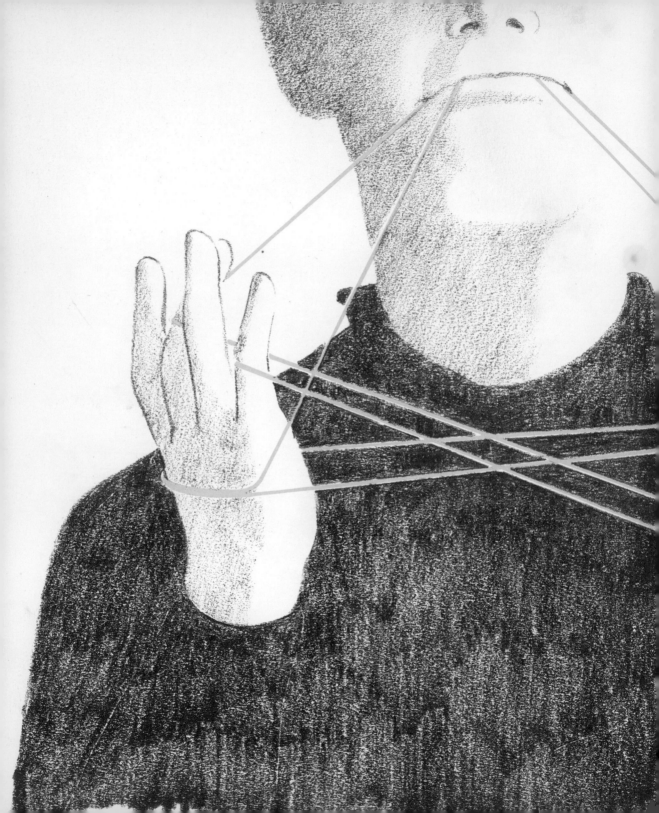

There are many tiny muscles in the fingers, thumb, and palm of your hand.

Each has a special job to do: to push this way, or to pull that way; to close the hand or to open it; to bend the thumb toward the palm, or to extend it from the palm.

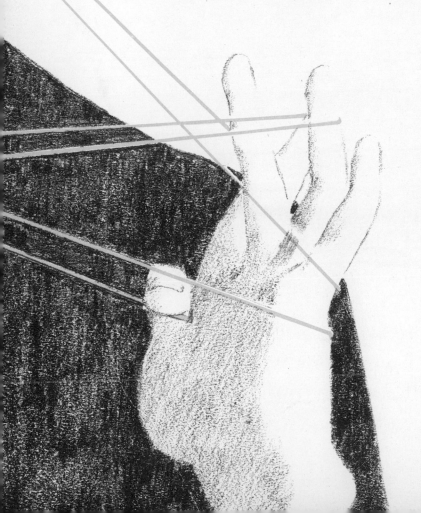

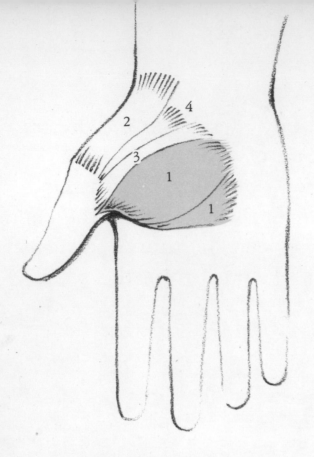

The thumb separates man from all other
creatures and places him above them, be-
cause it allows him many more actions
and abilities.

Just try to write with a pencil, button your
coat, or comb your hair without using your
thumb; you'll see how important it is. For
it is able to work *against* your four fingers.

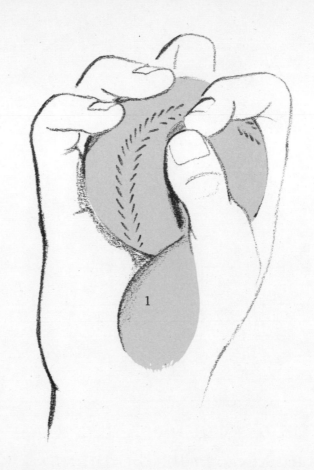

Muscle No. 1 of the thumb is very strong. It
  forms the heavy part of your thumb which
  sits in the palm.
It pulls the thumb toward the hand.
This muscle is necessary to get a good grip
  on an object.

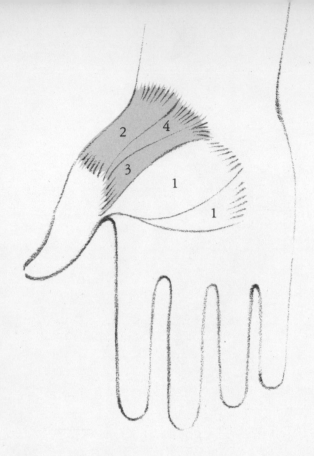

The thumb can reach and touch any finger.
Muscle No. 2 pulls the thumb toward the
    hand and can move it from side to side
    and backward.
Muscle No. 3 helps muscle No. 2.
Muscle No. 4 pulls the thumb away from the
    hand.
Of course, the thumb has other muscles, but
    these are the most important ones.

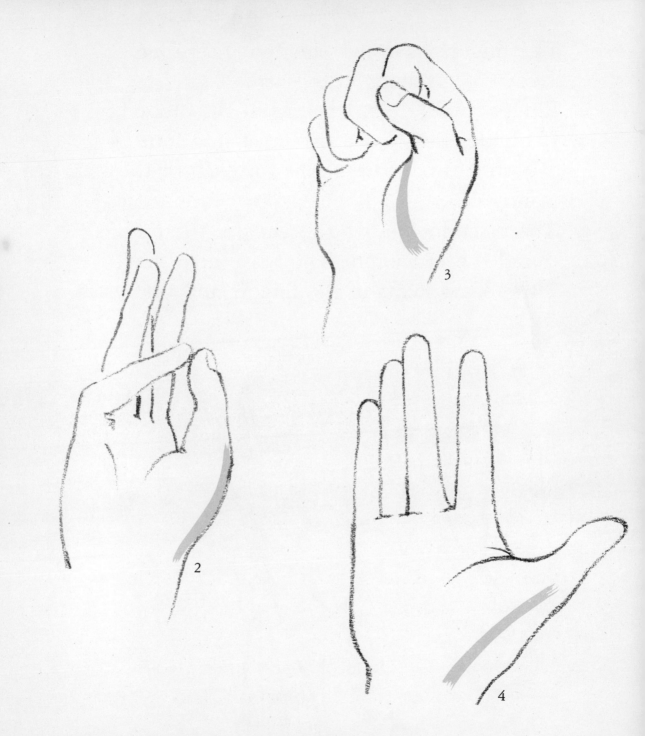

2

3

4

The fingers have muscles too. These have
their beginnings in the arm.
Finger muscle No. 1 begins at the elbow!
It divides just above the wrist into four
branches called *tendons* for each of the
fingers.
These tendons move the ends of the fingers,
and the last joints. They also help move
the other joints of the fingers and the wrist.

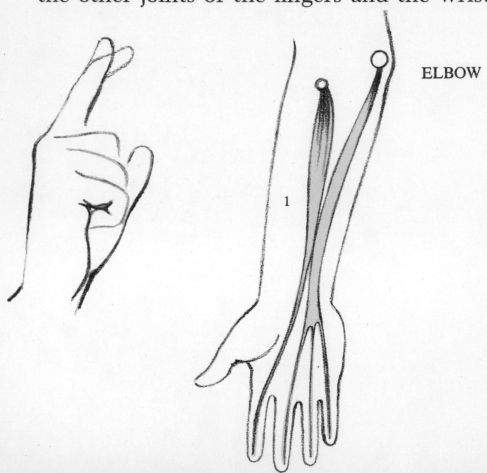

ELBOW

1

Finger muscle No. 2 also begins at the elbow
and divides into tendons for each of the
fingers.
These tendons move the first and middle
joints.

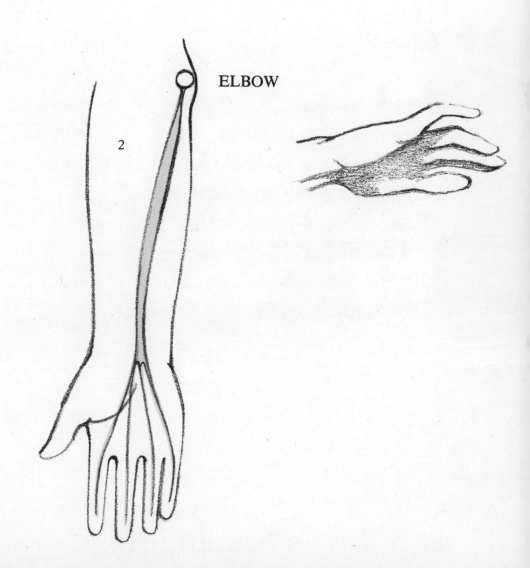

ELBOW

2

Finger muscles No. 3 and No. 4 also begin at
the elbow. They divide into powerful
tendons which control the first joints of
your fingers, nearest the palm.
Muscle No. 4 gives an extra tendon to the
little finger.
Muscle No. 5 is an extra-strong tendon for
the index finger.

3

4

5

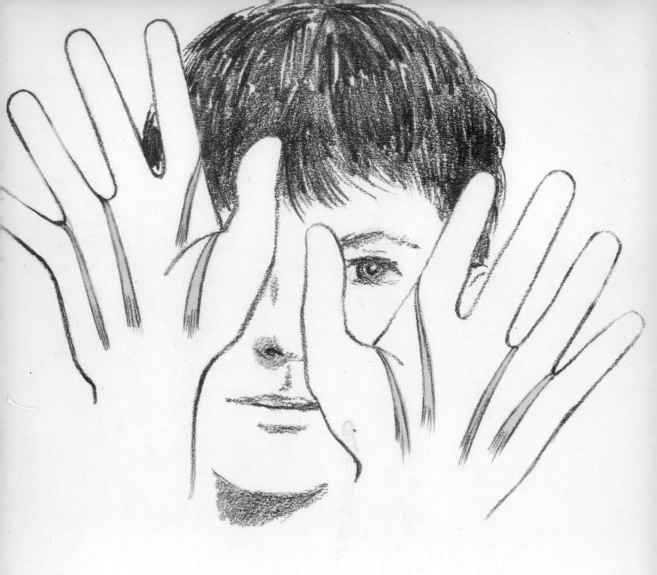

Then there are the muscles of the hand itself.
The four muscles of the palm are called the
  palmar muscles.
Palmar muscles spread your fingers apart.

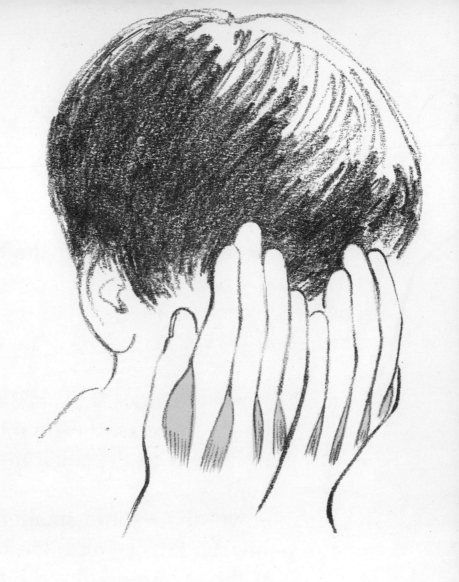

The four muscles of the back of the hand
are called the *dorsal* muscles.
Dorsal muscles bring your fingers together.

Nerves are thin cords which carry messages
    to and from the brain.
There are three main nerves of the hand:
    The *median* nerve,
    The *ulnar* nerve, and
    The *radial* nerve.

The median nerve divides into smaller nerves
    of the palm, the fingers, the thumb, and
    one special branch to the thick muscle pad
    of the thumb.
The ulnar nerve divides into smaller nerves
    of the palm, the fingers, and one branch to
    the side of the palm opposite the thumb.
The radial nerve divides into branches which
    go to the back of the fingers.

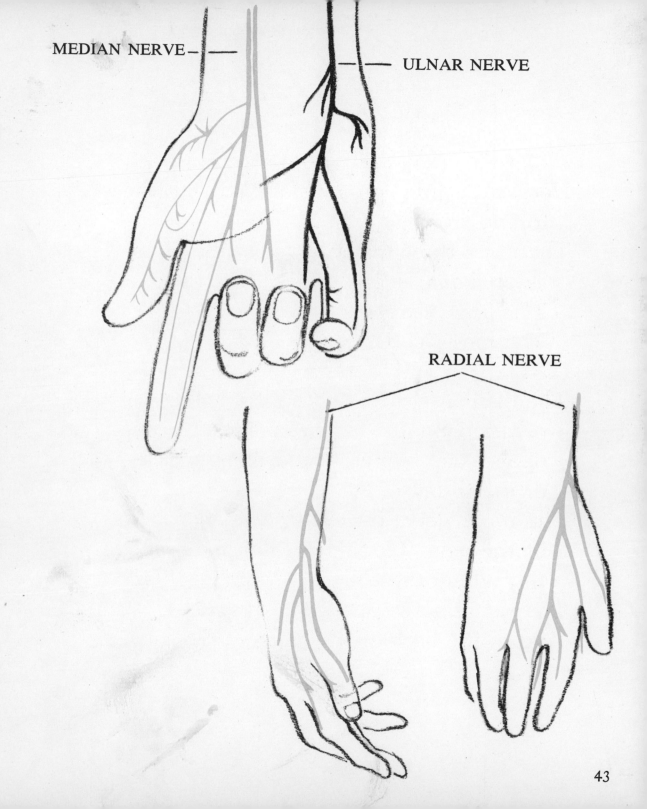

MEDIAN NERVE

ULNAR NERVE

RADIAL NERVE

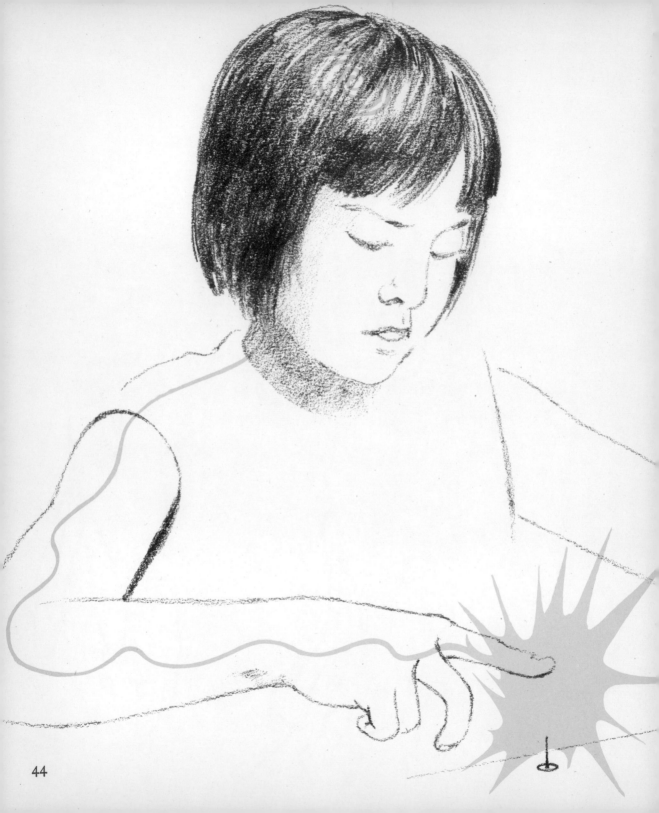

The muscles of your hand answer, and pull your finger from the tack in a split second. Nerves tell your brain the difference between hot and cold, rough and smooth, wet and dry.

If you are right-handed, the left side of your brain controls and instructs your hand. If you are left-handed, the right side of your brain is the boss.

Arteries and *veins* are thin tubes which carry
blood to all parts of your body.
There are two sets of arteries in each hand.
One set carries the blood to the palm of the
hand. These are called the *palmar* arteries.
The other set carries blood to the back of
your hand. These are called the *dorsal*
arteries.

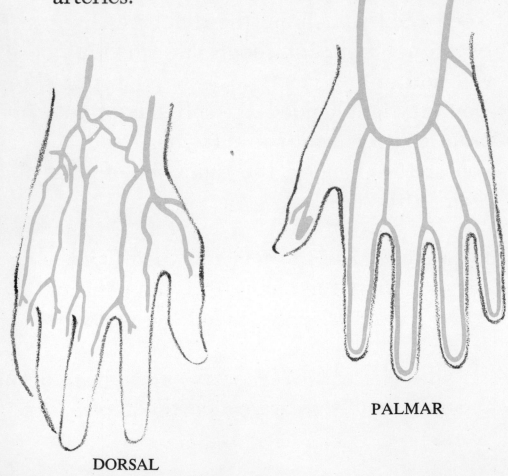

PALMAR

DORSAL

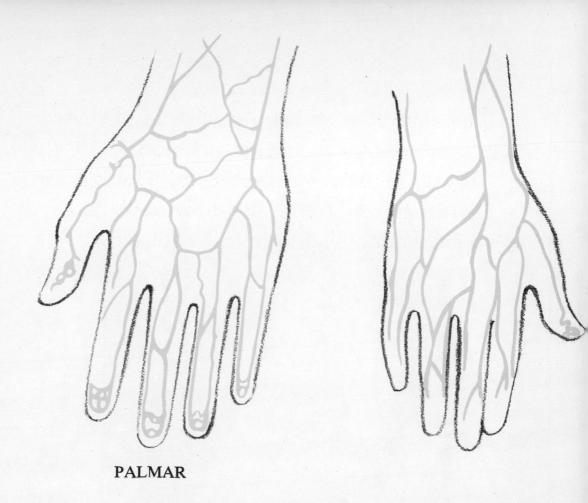

PALMAR

There are two sets of veins in each hand.
One set carries the blood from the palm of
    your hand. These are called the *palmar*
    veins.
The other set carries blood from the back of
    your hand. These are called the *dorsal*
    veins.

The skin of your hand covers all of these bones, muscles, nerves, arteries, and veins. Extremely hard layers of skin, which grow very slowly, form your fingernails.

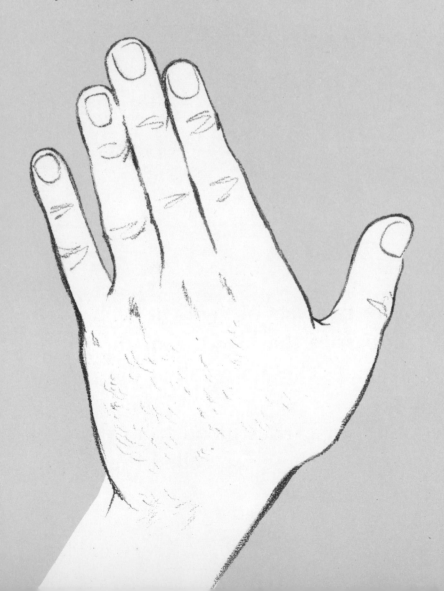

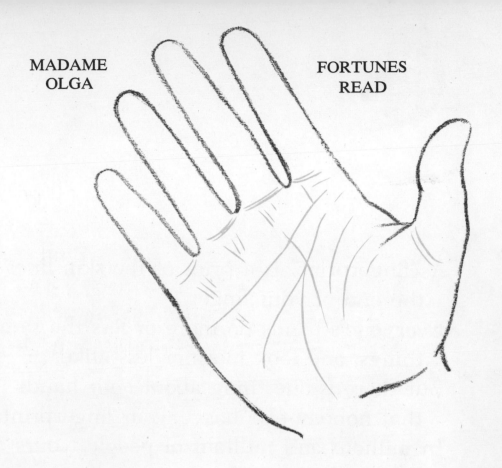

MADAME
OLGA

FORTUNES
READ

There are tiny hairs on the back of your
   hand, but none on the palm of your hand.
When you look at your palm, you see many
   tiny lines in the skin. Some people have
   names for these lines: "heart line," "life
   line," "marriage line," etc. They believe
   that your future can be read in these lines.

A "fingerprint" is a print of the skin lines on
   the end of your finger.
Everyone's hands do more or less the same
   things, and look more or less alike.
But there is one thing about *your* hands
   that nobody else has ... your fingerprints.
In millions and millions of people, yours are
   the only fingerprints which are *you*, an-
   other wonderful thing about that marvelous
   instrument, the human hand.

Index

E1